Groundwork

Also by Robert Morgan

POETRY

Zirconia Poems
Red Owl
Land Diving
Trunk & Thicket
Groundwork
Bronze Age
At the Edge of the Orchard Country
Sigodlin
Green River: New and Selected Poems
Wild Peavines
Topsoil Road
The Strange Attractor: New and Selected Poems

FICTION

The Blue Valleys
The Mountains Won't Remember Us
The Hinterlands
The Truest Pleasure
The Balm of Gilead Tree: New and Selected Stories
Gap Creek
This Rock
Brave Enemies

NONFICTION

Good Measure: Essays, Interviews, and Notes on Poetry
Boone: A Biography

Groundwork

by Robert Morgan

Gnomon Press

Copyright © 1979, 2007 by Robert Morgan
LCCN 79-55810
ISBN-10: 0-917788-21-4
ISBN-13: 978-0-917788-21-5 PAPER &
ISBN 0-917788-22-2 CLOTH

SECOND PRINTING WITH REVISIONS

Cover Art by Leah Palmer Preiss

Published by
GNOMON PRESS
P.O. Box 475
FRANKFORT, KY 40602-0475
http://www.gnomonpress.com/

for William Matthews

CONTENTS

The Hollow   1
Blue Ridge   2
Fear   3
Plankroad   4
Huckleberry Bald   6
Appalachian Trail   7
Mountain Bride   8
The Flying Snake   10
Lost Flower   12
Real and Ethereal   13
Galacker   14
Sport   16
Otis   17
Snowlight   18
Death Crown   19
Canning Time   20
Burnoff   22
When the Ambulance Came   23
Slop Bucket   25
Walnutry   26
Baptism of Fire   28
Bean Money   31
Huckleberries   32
Reuben's Cabin   34
Upstairs at the Country Store   36

Wallowing   38
Bricking the Church   39
Tear Bottle   40
Burning the Hornet's Nest   41
Milksick Pen   42
Smokehouse Dirt   43
Blackberries   44
Pigeon Loft   45
Mountain Page   47
Zircon Pit   49
Secret Pleasures   50
Den Tree   51
Devil's Courthouse   52
Trash   54
Praying Through   55

ACKNOWLEDGMENTS

Many of these poems were first printed in the following journals: *Iowa Review, The Small Farm, Poetry, The Cornell Review, Choice, New Lazarus Review, Attaboy!, The Grapevine, Hollow Spring Review, Vanderbilt Poetry Review, The Yale Review, Moosehead Review, Parnassus, Puddingstone, Southern Poetry Review, Poetry Now, The Chowder Review,* and *The Country Journal.*

'Lost Flower,' 'Pigeon Loft,' 'Zircon Pit,' and 'Secret Pleasures' first appeared in *Poetry.*

'Blue Ridge' and 'Blackberries' were first published in *New Directions 26.*

'Reuben's Cabin' was reprinted in *Travelling America with Today's Poets,* ed. David Kherdian, Macmillan, 1977.

'Mountain Bride' was reprinted in *A Geography of Poets,* ed. Edward Field, Bantam Books, 1979.

Several poems were first printed in a special issue of *The Small Farm.*

Publication of the first edition of this book was supported in part by a grant from the National Endowment for the Arts, a federal agency.

Thanks to Robert West for his help with this edition.

THE HOLLOW

First travelers to the coves of the Blue Ridge
up near the headsprings,
found no trails between
the cabin clearings. Each bit
of acreage along its branch
opened like an island inside the wilderness,
with paths to water and to the turnip patch
always stopping at the margin where
a groundhog sunned its gob of fur.
The children chewed tobacco or drank corn,
when someone picked his way
out through the thickets to obtain some.
Their best diversion of all, their most
accomplished: watching the mountain haze, the blue
haunt overhead that cooled
and lulled even the August sun
and lay out along the slopes like
a smoke of silence, an incense of their
lifelong vigil between the unstoned graves
and the wormy appletree, a screen
sent up from the oaks and hickories
to keep them hidden from disease
and god and government, and even time.

BLUE RIDGE

The divide is sharp as a mule's back,
parts rainfall at the rim
and forwards it on.
The defining ridge, flanked
by higher, separate peaks, wanders
itself unbroken, wind-plucked,
running out
through mists and rhododendrons,
above hemlocks and dripping ledges,
the ground charged with
a current of clear water.
Here a spring has first choice,
the first gathering of moisture, a valve
feeding out evenly
far from the sweet thrusting
into estuaries, the sloughs of rich
chemistry,
and dissipation in tidal flats.
Here is no accumulation.
At the farthest boundary of
the ocean's magnet
water gathers itself from
the dirt speaking cold and clear.

FEAR

Up here in the hemlock hollow
below the crag,
off the haulroad and trail, we live
close to the fire, scared
of falling trees and big wind,
wildcats, lightning,
afraid of snakes and water, deep snow.
There is no medicine against the horror
of shade near the family burial patch.
A flea circus of dust thrown
up in the yard means
the haints are near
and ghosties roost like cocoons
in the appletree. I've seen bones
underground burn like filaments
when passed over by highwires from town,
in torment with
the suffering of the elements.
Everybody knows the waterfall is
haunted by a woman
strangled in her wedding dress back then;
mushrooms are the fingers
of the dead reaching through
and crickets their moving eyes.
Trash around the spring means one
has tried to get back in there.

PLANKROAD

Besides the Indian trails and a crude wagon trace
the first way into the mountains from the south
was a narrow gauge set of timbers on the ground
with rough boards nailed across. The clatter
of that lumber echoed off the mountains' wall
as teams and carriages from Charleston
labored up along the Saluda and into the dark
hollows, ascending out of the heat. Those sleepers
rumbled like trolls under their load and
wallowed in the spring mud, drumming to the
jumpoffs and high ledges a warning: see

> maples unfurl and sail on light into spring,
> see higher up the oaks like ragged beggars carrying
> diamonds of sap to translate into green.
> The fullness has come to the cucumber trees
> along the upcountry creek where floods scoured
> the underbrush a few weeks ago. The new growth
> tinctures light where sun has made the soil
> ethereal in leaves. And solar wind takes flesh
> in kalmia and chinquapin.

The millionaires from Charleston and
Atlanta built their mansions in the pines
at Flat Rock, and returned each year along
the wooden bridge to cool among the columns
and hemlocks, and worship in their private chapel.
They bought poultry and time from my forebears.
Observe the proficiency of sprouts
trading in the commissary of mud, now as
back when they grumbled from the tollhouse near
Traveler's Rest up to the Gap. Natives

walked their planks into the outlands.
The wood quickly weathered and warped where
it stilted across the hungry water
and parted thickets.
The platforms snapped in cloudbursts
and fungus in the lowspots ate
the flooring like venison. Then
they had their Negroes and Irishmen
dig and drag a locomotive into the mountains.

HUCKLEBERRY BALD

Some highest peaks and ridges are
kept bare of trees and even rhododendrons by
violent winds on the headflanks.
Coming up the final slope spruce get
runted and thin out to shrubs, then
at the top just a few low bushes
hug the spots of ground
and huddle in the lees of rock.
Within inches of the moss their berries
darken like droplets of the essence
of the Blue Ridge — a giant dew
higher than the seep-springs —
for bear and grouse and bees.
Some think the Indians cleared these
lofty fields and planted out the
tiny orchards of whortle to be polished by
storms, or that lightning-scalds or
aphid-blight stripped the peaks for summer
pasturage by elk and deer.
At this elevation only playing close
and rooting deep can take the blasts
of upper streams: lichen, grass, and rockfern,
and little fruit trees that sneak along
the rim away from the prevailing whip
to shake their cool seeds at the sun.

APPALACHIAN TRAIL

Feeds on cloud along the humps,
climbing out of somnolence
of smog and crawling heat
to the wind-glazed acres then

dropping back into the gap,
accurate to horizon.
Goes ditching the spine of the divide,
accessible to overlooks and thickets.

Follows the high resolution of land nowhere
choosing sides, fence sitter,
mugwumping arctic flora
stranded here since the ice age

and dorsal flanks mulched by fogs
in highvolt storms wrecking from the Gulf.
Lichens attach their crampons to rocks
like flames sucking at a log

and height-stunted species grip
the precincts lean of oxygen.
Defines the
land's cutting edge.

MOUNTAIN BRIDE

They say Revis found a flatrock
on the ridge just
perfect for a natural hearth,
and built his cabin with a stick

and clay chimney right over it.
On their wedding night he lit
the fireplace to dry away the mountain
chill of late spring, and flung on

applewood to dye
the room with molten color while
he and Martha that was a Parrish
warmed the sheets between the tick

stuffed with leaves and its feather
cover. Under that wide hearth
a nest of rattlers,
they'll knot a hundred together,

had wintered and were coming awake.
The warming rock
flushed them out early.
It was she

who wakened to their singing near
the embers and roused him to go look.
Before he reached the fire
more than a dozen struck

and he died yelling her to stay
on the big four-poster.
Her uncle coming up the hollow
with a gift bearham two days later

found her shivering there
marooned above a pool
of hungry snakes,
and the body beginning to swell.

THE FLYING SNAKE

The giant rattler that lived in
the rocks above the Gap Road
watched teams and passing
riders from its summer ledge,
almost invisible in moss.
If bothered it could drain
its black feet into a crevice
or, provoked, spring on a horse or driver,
raking the neck with its
loaded fangs and flopping off
into the brush below the trace
before one had mastered
panic enough to
shoot the leg-sized whip of lightning.
Four settlers had died, and many
mules and oxen.
Even the old Cherokee formula
of singing the snake its own song
was useless if it struck before seen.
Once a posse climbed up in the cliffs
and shot a dozen small ones but
the old killer sank back
into the mountain, and seemed
to know just like a crow if one
was coming armed.
It was Great-grandpa as a youth
who thought of tying his seine net
around the yoke and under the chests
of his steers, and drove standing
in the wagon with a shotgun in the hay.
That cool August noon the jarflies
sang like rattlers in the trees

and ripe huckleberries
sweetened the air.
Flying squirrels swept
in the high branches of the oaks, and
way down the valley he could hear
Aunt Tildy's chickens
routed by a hawk.
Coming near the rocks he crouched
to cock the gun and let the team
nose slowly into the shivering
spots of sunlight.
He heard the cold thunder necklace fling
off the shelf above and as it caught
in the webbing by its barbs he
just had time, before it
thrashed free, to raise the
barrel and cut the jewelled blur in two.
The head piece bit a rock
and soaked the ground with venom.
The tail twitched on for hours
like something dreaming.
The two halves filled a half bushel
and he sewed the sixteen rattles to his hat.
Years later he'd imagine spiders
falling from the sky like snowflakes,
and mad dogs and angels in storms,
and once in a nightmare he shot
by mistake Jesus as he came
through the east in Rapture light.

LOST FLOWER

Old Asa Gray from Harvard looked high
in the mountains for the shortia
that Michaux had discovered and plucked
on the Blue Ridge and dried for his collection
back in France almost a century before.
No botanist had seen its bloom, nor
knew where to climb for the dazzling beds
the Frenchman had extolled in his journal.
Professor Gray named it *shortia galacifolia* for
a friend and sent assistants every summer
to the highlands to explore the summits
for the herb that had no relative except
one cherished breed in China,
a sacred mountain flower.
But when they found the shortia abloom
in oriental profusion all over the south
flank of Transylvania County late in the last
century, it gloried slopes lower
than expected, haunting just above the coves
at the edge of South Carolina and in the shade
of heavy woods, curd-white and shy in the
trash of the forest floor, smaller than its
Chinese twin, and called by neighbors
the Oconee Bell for where it rang quiet
on the lower elevations, no higher
than the best-fed springs.

REAL AND ETHEREAL

Called the 'highest steamboat line
in America' they operated *The Mountain
Lily* on the French Broad back in
the 80's. The only navigable
stretch, from Fletcher to Brevard,
rose in the spring too
sassy to negotiate, and by
midsummer thinned so shallow the hull
scraped on rocky bottom.
The muddy cartway on the hills
was more reliable.
Not even jetties built
to deepen and narrow the channel
proved a remedy.
There's a picture someone made
of the sidewheeler stranded on mud
near the bend at Arden,
swaybacked and listing, stack
tilted like a gun.
Not so much a floating palace
as a tenement or bunkhouse
on a barge. They
salvaged the motor
and dismantled the rest for lumber —
some of the planks in Horse Shoe Church
once steamed through the gap
into the stadium of mountains
with the Sunday bell warning of departure.

GALACKER: THE GALAX GATHERER

Along in late November after at least
one hard freeze, old man Revis took his sacks
along the creekbank and hindledges of
the cove to find a last autumn in the beds
and couches of the woods between the wagon
trace and the crest of the divide from its
north exposure. And there plucked on hands and
knees among the winter trash the cover
of this creeping herb, its evergreen
cut from jade and plated bronze, lacquered,
and wired deep in the mould. Each leaf had been
polished and dusted, teeth filed on the edges.
You rarely notice the milky blossoms
because of undergrowth, only the black
leaves in winter sparkling. Those blessed by
coldest wind spitshine the floor maroon,
always clear of snow except where the roots
of an oak mop up the seepage and scrub
the water table bare. His thick hands
cropped and stuffed the mirror greens in bags,
but not with pressure as for cowbedding.
That night by the fire he'd tie the best in
booklets for shipping north, and rest, waiting
for his pay till after New Year's, two bits
per thousand.

        In the gloomy latter days
of a depression year I root on the
woods floor for the oiled metals, knees
in mud, hands rotten with cold, careful as
a numismatist foraging the flanks
of the hollow, not for the clabber
of the shaded blossoms nor pale salad
growth, but to forward out in sewn wreaths
and pamphlets of commemoration,
the pages of this local archaic herb.

SPORT

The mink that soaked itself into
my grandma's chickenhouse
must have worked quick and silent
for no one heard a cackle in the night.
But going out to feed and gather eggs
she felt the slab-shack quiet
and saw the empty yard.
The door swung back on leather hinges to let
sunlight find them on the wet
red floor, the faithful layers
raised from biddies,
each neck slit where he took
a sip, then plucked another down
from the roost, sampling all forty-six
to leave draining on the dirt
otherwise untouched — their eyes
stretching to the razored dark —
before he osmosed back into the night.
They cleaned and singed all morning
and had chicken twice that day,
carrying the rest to neighbors.
The blood-soaked ground they
shoveled out into the seedbed
pelted with flies. My father caught
a mink that winter, in the branch below
the barn, that tried to gnaw
its foot off in the trap
but drowned, teeth frozen in the joint.

OTIS

When the pistol rang among
the circle of admiring boys
(Sylvan had it from his father's
closet) out near the milkgap,
it was Sylvan who hollered, 'I'm
shot,' and fell on the grass
clawing neck and chest.
But as they watched his throes
in horror Otis said,
'No, Sylvan, I'm the one it hit,'
and they saw blood soaking out
above his belt. The doctor rode
over from Saluda and operated half the night
on the kitchen table to find
the ball and sew him back.
But the wound drained faulty,
and after two days' swelling,
black pain and white
lipped prayer, Otis died
at sunrise. The last time
I saw Sylvan he was sheriff
of Saluda, more than eighty, still
a talker, always laughing louder,
longer than his listener.

SNOWLIGHT

Grandpa knew for certain it would snow
if he went out early to grind
his coffee in the backporch mill
and saw the glow behind the
mountain steady and close
as lighted cities.
He thought snow an electrical
condition of the air, a discharge like
St. Elmo's fire on the high
peaks that spilled down and
coated everything with angelic smuts,
fleshing the limbs of a dead pine
so they smoked and flared in the
early sun, giving body to the light
after its long descent to
suffer weight among the branches.
Stirred by shadows on the sun
and currents in the ground
the aura signalled its approach.
Before evening we'd see the wind
charged and wrestling its host of sparks.

DEATH CROWN

In the old days back when
one especially worthy lay dying
for months, they
say the feathers in the pillow would
knit themselves into a crown
that those attending felt in perfect
fit around the honored head.
The feather band they took to be
certain sign of another crown,
the saints and elders of the church,
the Deep Water Baptists said.
I've seen one unwrapped from its
cloth in the attic, the down
woven perfect and tight for
over a century, shiny but
soft and light almost as light.

CANNING TIME

The floor was muddy with the juice of peaches
and my mother's thumb, bandaged for the slicing,
watersobbed. She and Aunt Wessie skinned
bushels that day, fat Georgia Belles
slit streaming into the pot. Their knives
paid out limp bands onto the heap
of parings. It took care to pack the jars,
reaching in to stack the halves
firm without bruising, and lowering
the heavy racks into the boiler already
trembling with steam, the stove malignant
in heat. As Wessie wiped her face
the kitchen sweated its sweet filth.
In that hell they sealed the quickly browning
flesh in capsules of honey, making crystals
of separate air across the vacuums.
The heat and pressure were enough to grow
diamonds as they measured hot
syrup into quarts. By supper the last jar
was set on the counter to cool
into isolation. Later in the night
each little urn would pop as it
achieved its private atmosphere and
we cooled into sleep, the stove now
neutral. The stones already
pecked clean in the yard were free to try
again for the sun. The orchard meat fixed in
cells would be taken down cellar in the
morning to stay gold like specimens
set out and labelled, a vegetal
battery we'd hook up later. The women

too tired to rest easily think of
the treasure they've laid up today
for preservation at coffin level, down there
where moth and rust and worms corrupt,
a first foundation of shells to be
fired at the winter's muddy back.

BURNOFF

Come spring we hell the high field,
cremating brush cities and stubble.
One spark touched upwind
pours out across the acres popping
joints of old weeds and running
every fuse of vine to root. The firesheet
spreads along the ground a rough tide
to the pasture break.
See the effigies of summer pass
like shadows through the pyre and ascend
dropping letters that melt
in the backwash of ash.
As though the conflagration summons
dirt syrup and fire ink out of clay
to irrigate anemic soil
and pave the slope tar-black.
The shadow will need to be turned
like frying ham, sweet with
baked larvae, wormeggs, roots.
We rub the season's minstrel char
on skin, and ask the land to hold its
charge until we plug in seeds.
The cinders, potash, fire manure,
will crawl out again
from caustic rubble
into green corridors, upper rooms,
following the smoke castles
thrown into the trees.

WHEN THE AMBULANCE CAME

When the ambulance came for Grandma
that day in Easter snow
I watched them lift the stretcher
through the kitchen door.

One attendant stood in mud by
the steps where we threw the
dishwater and leftovers for the chickens:
I saw a piece of cabbage stick on

his shoe. Another wet
his glasses in the droplets
from the eave that stained the sheet as they
lowered her strapped to a tray

into the wailing oven.
Grandma had sat wrapped in the corner
for weeks protesting her
health before screaming.

Her head shaved and sawed open in Charlotte
yielded an egg-sized tumor.
The tracks where they backed across the yard
were still legible after the funeral

as the green seeped back into the stubble
over the cesspool.
That winter she had taken me to rake
leaves for cowbedding with a forked

stick in the woods above the barn.
I remember how naked the ground looked where
she gathered its cover into sacks,
and how the driver cursed the torn

roads over the mountain
when he slammed the spattered door
on her seventy years
of staying home.

SLOP BUCKET

Fumes from the cabinet under the sink
mingle ferment, sour and rot.
Once a paint-bucket streaked with black
enamel over the galvanized frost, but

crusted now with long-dried slop
almost transparent set with scabs
baked on daily by warming at
the stove before carrying out to the squeal.

A pone sops in collard grease,
beets purpling over sour milk,
membranes of lettuce,
heaped on sifters of bran and blinky swill.

Spirits cook in the undercupboard there
noticed only at night
at family altar when the odors
scrimmage along the floor like ghosts of appetite.

WALNUTRY

When walnuts grew in stands like oak
or hickory in some mountain coves
and the timber market lay
over trails and feisty creeks,
some cut their big nut groves the same
as pine, and sawed out planks for
porches, barns, even hogpens.
With never stain nor varnish they
took the weather for a century,
growing stronger, like cement.
The seasoning took twenty years.
They didn't need the meat as
long as there were chestnuts.
Where the cows had rubbed
their stalls shone like mirrors.

Rainy Sundays in late fall my father
took the egg basket out to the walnut
in the chicken lot and gathered
half a bushel. The hull ink
tanned his palms.
Inside he set them on the hearth
and peeled the sooty rinds off
into the fire. They
censed the house with raw
fumes. He sat there all afternoon
on the warm rock cracking with
his mason's hammer, holding the shells
on end so they split clean,
working careful as a sculptor
to get the little figures of meat
intact from their molds,

and dealt the pieces to Sister
and me for hours while rain
flared on the windows and burst in the fire
compacting brighter on the diet
of shells. That night I'd throw up
the oily seeds gluttoned all evening,
and remember again the ground
under the big walnut
purged bare by the drip
and dissolution of
the tree's powerful bile.

BAPTISM OF FIRE

'A moonpie and a yaller dope,' Gondan
ordered every noon when Daddy took
the pickup down to the diner on the highway
for our lunch. We ate in the weeds
crowding to the shade of a wild cherry:
hotdogs, Pepsis, a tube of peanuts each.
But Gondan, who professed to preach when
one of the ridge churches lent him
its pulpit, sat alone in the sun
and argued to all and the August heat his doctrine.
'The Book says a man's not sanctified until
he has the Baptism, until he has the fire,'
he grinned and pulled on the tall orange drink.
'It says a man can fall again without
he's washed by the Ghost of fire,' louder,
daring any Washfoot Baptist in the group
to dispute him. The girls adjusted cutoff jeans
and looked away toward the trees
by the creek where they'd go with one
of the older boys before the afternoon
was done. Once Old Man Bane, who picked our
beans to supplement his pension from the
Spanish American War and lived in semi-deafness,
ventured that the only cleansing to
count was water symbolic of the Blood,
to get to heaven. Gondan, still chewing the
moonpie and shaking with excitement, yelled,
'The Word says it takes the Baptism of Fire
to see the Kingdom, and anyone tells it different's
a cockeyed liar.' None challenged him; if
prodded further he would start to fight and

shout and laugh at once. When teased outside
the cottonmill one night he rolled himself
through a big puddle until they stopped him.
We sat crusted with sweatsalt in
the stingy shade. The boys flicked peanuts
at a cricket and Junior, with perfect aim, sent
one into Linda's shorts. The beanrows wobbled
and shivered in the clear flames and
luffed like sails when a breeze
passed on the vines already yellow with
maturity. It would be schooltime soon
and we were saving to buy new clothes.
Gondan wore his suitcoat in the field no
matter what the weather, its collar
ripening with damp and smut spores.
The clods glared harsh as ice and brimstone.
'But with that final bath of fire
you're insured against hell and feel
a great big tin tub of honey dumped all
over your soul.' He volunteered once for
the mission field, but the office in Raleigh
rejected him for lack of education.
No church in the valley would give him
the call to be its pastor, and the mill had
fired him for provoking quarrels.
'Anyone that ain't rubbed clean by
purifying flame better get his asbestos suit,'
he finished and threw the bottle into the brush,
heading for the scorched rows to pick
silently the rest of the day. Daddy called
Gondan the slowest hand he'd ever hired,

and wouldn't have kept him on except a man
of the Lord could not be left to starve.
Replacing the bottles neatly in their crate
on the tailgate we followed reluctantly
back into the furnace of vines,
comforted by meager shadows and the wind
that pushed the tangled field and all its
load of weeds and riggings into autumn.

BEAN MONEY

Back from the market late with a watermelon
and his bib-pocket full of cash
my father shoved a fist of back-pay
for the summer at me, the yield from
digging holes and tying strings,
lugging hampers in the rain with heat rash,
stings and blisters. In my room I'd sit
with dirty feet and sweat-ripe skin
on the sheets and unwad the damp bills
to press in stacks like pages of a ledger
of the hot days, the green and gray ink
more lasting than sunburn or calluses,
and telling of my labor with a one-eye
lit pyramid. I collated
and banded the leaves in bundles
and counted out the coins like next year's
seeds into the old tobacco pouch.
That consecrated metal was an abstract
drawn off the soil and sweat and
cast into a jewelry of value.
I meant those struck emblems to act
as compact fuel, like nuclear pellets,
to power my long excursion out of the sun
and beyond the ridges, and put
them all in a paper box above the closet
door to trade later; the young summers
become signs to be translated
again into paper, ink and paper,
in the cool timeless leisure I saw
while washing my feet on the back steps
and spitting melon seeds
into the cricket-haunted dark.

HUCKLEBERRIES

The walkingstick emerged articulate
on the twig near F. A.'s fingertip.
It flies faster than a hummingbird, he said,
pushed by its rows of thorns.

Never trust the innocent twig in high
berry country; it may be stingworm,
snake or walkingstick.

And then I heard the buzz that seemed
to fill the woods with charge.
July sweat dripped clear as venom
into my vision and stung.
Just a jarfly, he assured. A rattler
wouldn't go on so long or loud.

Forest litter dry as ashes. Something
rang in the wet masonry of the spine.
A stream wrote itself across the logging
trail. The berries so few, so tedious
to gather, seemed to reflect little skies
the size of sinkers. They burst
in spores of pure color.
We passed the overhanging rocks
where seepage bled on moss.

That's where the painter hid, F. A. recalled,
the one that stole the babies from
the settlement. It smelled the
mothers' milk for miles and knew
a baby's cry. Once Alice Jeeter left
her newborn on the porch to go inside

for a pan to shell more peas in; she heard
a thud and rush and ran out
to see the black fiend vanish
with the baby into brush.

After that a posse dogged its trail
up here and covered the den all day and night
until starvation drew the big cat out. They planted it
with a hundred bullets. A pile
of infant bones was found puked up
and half-buried in one corner of the hole.

Before midday we knew enough to take
our homewoven baskets and descend
the trail around The Mare Slide, feverish
with concentration on the bushes and heat.

The closework: as sun getting dew
out of thickets, picking old burns
and outcroppings, kneeling in stooplabor
among the burrows and soaking
up chiggers and ticks, to count
the manybeaded treasure into the bucket
for crisping in the spring at noon.
The morning has been said and won,
hands bloody with sweet sun.

REUBEN'S CABIN

Looked stitched together and
patched with warping Pepsi signs,
stilted to the ridge.
The rathides hung out to cure
under the eaves could have been
part of his random repair.
In the warm months he'd
sit by the river for days, pole
stuck in the mud, hunched
beneath the tarp thrown
on a makeshift frame for wet weather.
That's why collectors rarely
found him when they climbed up to
his roughly-scaffolded roost.
The story had it the girl he
married in the low country
went bad, and none of the children
long since gone were
conceived in his bed.
During the first World War, Reuben
hid in the family's attic, then
after the armistice snuck out
and arrived at the depot
in uniform. Look, I've heard
Reuben rolled his cornbread
in little pills to eat and seen
him cuss my grandpa once when
he got up to testify. His wife
gone to hell, his piles,
the dirty pension.

Reuben, what were you thinking
those long hours in the mud by
the catfish waters while
the schoolbus passed and returned?
The tarpaper on your roof has flown
down into the trees along the creek.
Your traps' jaws are
locked by rust where they hang
along the ridgepole and squirrels
have stolen all the innards from
your smelly couch. What
are you thinking now in the
silence circling up near Buzzard Rock?

UPSTAIRS AT THE COUNTRY STORE

The only public place besides
the church and school and post office
in our valley was the store down
at the crossroads. Above its display
case of troutflies and cartridges, the cookies
soaked in their sealed jar.
A pistol dangled on its lanyard
behind the counter and new steel traps
flashed their greased tongues.

Paved with bottlecaps, the yard
threw its glare in the window
over the drink cooler and the dead
stove where the checker players
huddled in winter,
to find the banks of cans roosting on
the shelves. Frost appeared from within and
thickened on the chocolate skin
of a popsicle. Breath made it
go away leaving the shell wet as
the icebox. The ground underneath
the bench outside wore
intimate where talkers
slouched in warm weather.

Out back the shed held hay and shorts
and dairy-feed, the tank for minnows,
air pump, wheelbarrows, seed, tomato slips
in season, and in the basement
eggs and butter we brought down
to trade. But the room remembered best
I never saw, the one reached by

the backstairs and always locked.
Nobody ever mentioned that attic around
the checkerboard or as they spat out front.

But often before going to sleep or
while hunting in the gloomy arbors I
would see the dusty upper room where the coffins
lay stacked like canoes,
some open for inspection of the silk
and lace pillows, craft of
polished wood, metal, or rich
brocade, waiting for the bereaved
family to come, anticipating their grief,
and ready to be carried down to truck
or wagon for the journey home
in the cool autumn night, or snowstorm,
or mid-summer morning while the corn
was being hoed and crows worried
above the hillpines. And after the
terrible service be launched again
into the cellar undercurrents
with no harbor but the weather.

WALLOWING

When Old Nell rolled in the bins
hollowed out of the pasture flats she
whinnied with the pleasure
as one ripened area of skin after
another whetted the firm ground,
shuddered and twisted to reach
itches on withers and rump.
She seemed more like a snake or worm there
on her back, often pulsing in coital
shiver like an amoeba.
I knew she scrubbed off fly eggs,
dung, dried blood from bites,
in the rasp of sand,
the emery submersion salving
harness galls and currying off sweat,
massaging the soreness of age.
Finding still neglected precincts
she'd press them with a snort to
dry grass at the lip of the wallow,
stoking and frisking hair roots,
and getting down into the trough
generate with friction a field of brushed
nerves. She indulged a third of her
hide at once to the bump and tickle,
running with the pasture on her back.
She thrashed the late summer dust
in a whirlpool, then
stood and shook herself of the dry
cloud and, smoking pure and free
as if new-born in the depression,
stepped onto the wide pasture.

BRICKING THE CHURCH

At the foot of Meetinghouse Hill
where once the white chapel
pointed among junipers and pulled
a wash of gravestones west,

they've buried the wooden snow that
answered sarvis in bloom
and early morning fogs, in brick,
a crust the same dull red

as clay in nearby gullies.
The little churchhouse now looks more
like a post office or school.
It's hard to find

among the brown winter slopes
or plowed fields of spring.
Brick was prestigious back when
they set their minds and savings to it.

They wanted to assert its form
and presence if not in stone
at least in hardened earth, urban weight,
as the white clapboards replaced

unpainted lumber which replaced
the logs of the original
where men brought their guns to preaching
and wolves answered the preacher.

The structure grows successive rings,
and as its doctrine softens
puts on a hard shell
for weathering this world.

TEAR BOTTLE

Find among the moulder of rocks and
encyclopedic composture this
morsel of grief. Where sun has
compounded and fire anatomized,

a dosage of bone ink
histories the rednecks and hoojers.
Bottles no ship but seas wept small
by saints of my childhood for law

and changes. Stone hollowed thin
as a testicle and tight as a seed
canteens a drop, real
to the fifth essence.

BURNING THE HORNET'S NEST

The great paper lantern in the appletree
does not come on at dark, is shaded
even from starlight. But waiting
until night you climb up into the belfry

of limbs and feel it near,
approach not jarring the branch
it's soldered to. A rancid
heat emanates from where

they sleep, a crackling like acid working.
Light the kerosene-soaked cob and jab
at the aperture. Burning, the fabric
eyeball seems even bigger. Jerking

outer layers catch and peel
upwards. Pellets drip out.
The sunflower heads of wet
larvae are reluctant, seethe

like juices and drop off whole post offices
of trout bait smoldering in the damp
weeds. Next morning survivors clamp
to the rags hanging around the empty socket.

MILKSICK PEN

If you come, in some cove or
hollow, on a fence around a patch
of brush and weeds and trees,
know that lot excludes
cattle for a reason. Somewhere
among the luxurious foliage
penned up with rails a
venomed vine threads out of
mould or a toxic leaf breathes shade.
No one knows which simple does
the murder-work, but
years ago they died who
drank the milk of cows that
grazed here. Protected
from the ax and herds by poison
the garden flourishes virgin.
I rest here, on an island
quiet as a graveyard, where
the weeds throw out their
sperm into the currents.
Drink the air of an orchard
purged, unfallen.

SMOKEHOUSE DIRT

The shadow of the meat-hung roof puddles
sterile as the site of Carthage. Rain will
lick away the savor in about
a century. The light cannot feel at

home on this ground for a while, nor rabbits
warm here at a hearth of vegetation.
The scald won't even
hold a crop of snow, but eats

away the lush crystals fast as heat.
Where the smoked ham sweated and fatback wept
its oils, and molasses cooked
down to plasma in jars, erosion

rubs brine in the wound same as a pissburn
in the pasture. The lye tub drooled its
whey also. Hunger has left a tear
track, recondite among the thickets.

BLACKBERRIES

Among the bloodfilled eyes
and towering vegetation,
invisible
traffic of chiggers.
Leaves bear ticks like hungry berries.
You dive in trampling mole runs
and spilling birdnests,
brush the fanged stems
to gather a few
with the blue jays and yellowjackets.
Wade into the snaky weeds as into a minefield.
Leaves have caught in the briars
and piled up a hive for rats
and spiders.
Quail leave in a snort.
The arching long-necked thickets
weigh with loads of shot
bright as caviar.

PIGEON LOFT

Kept to fight away the hawks from our pen
of fryers, they squabbled and mated
on the eaves of the crib and toolshed.
I imagined high Armageddons between our birds
and the death carriers from the woods.
They landed to peck for corn with the chickens,
cooed and groomed themselves
sleek as dolphins. Straw stuck pubic
through cracks and the small door
in the box nailed to the barn gable.

No matter how bloody after battle, or
storm-driven into other counties, they always
homed accurate as salmon to the crate
no bigger than a transformer where
they dallied out of reach of varmints.
Caked and chalked the ground below
their garret of heat.
Grandpa said they steered not by sun
or memory, or ear, but by instinct
from God to be messengers, like angels.
The night my uncle died in England one came
and lit on the porch railing in the light
from the window and later in the dark
till morning without moving.
They were my uncle's birds. That
same night my mother saw in a vision
his death in the burning B-17, and saw
the bird still there at daylight
on the spot where her brother used to sit.

They slept in the high dark, and dropped
out to soar at the stooping barbs,
alert to any whistle. So keen-eared that far above
the fields they heard the trucks down on the
highway and hogs grunting in other valleys,
airplanes in flight south of Greenville,
and listened to the lunge and plunder of
the Atlantic five-hundred miles to the east,
and the many voices beyond.

MOUNTAIN PAGE

I've seen the sky hang out its laundry
after a summer storm above the
headcreeks of the Saluda
and the vasty fornix fill to its summit
with boiling light.

My people came from South Carolina by
way of Mountain Page in the last century
and suffered here long enough
to build a church and leave
a dozen graves in the crab orchard.

One wasted years in search of
a secret lead mine the Cherokees
rumored was behind a cliff
on the back of Callahan
and tilting the rock northeast.

Another shunned his fields to dig for
gold the millionaires at Flat Rock
must have buried in the Civil War,
and found a few heathen graves
sealed in isinglass.

The church down here lasts
weathered like a pile of rocks and fungus
among the gullies. Pebbles in
the graveyard raise on pedestals of dirt.
Water drives east in a hurry

past the Old Fields of the Catawbas
and cones of sawdust left
burning when they took the big vegetables apart.
The roads back of Polk County
throw up smoke screens over August

and I stop to let their haunt blow
past and dew out in the weeds
while I prospect and dig and bury
expectations; my people
prayed and dug and failed here too.

ZIRCON PIT

Just below the crest of Meetinghouse Hill
I used to climb the apron of spoil
into a digging long abandoned. Leaves
and saplings hid the raw dirt and the hole,
half-filled in fall, fit like a nest
from which to drowse and look
down the steepness and keep watch
on my century. One of the high places.
I spent hours there in late winter,
warmed by leaves and the solartrap, just
out of the summit winds compressing
across the rim. Caught the best sun, the new light
of February when the mountains
pressed clean by snow began to twitch
and trickle. From that blind
I watched the mailman on the creekroad
hours before he reached our box.
The only gem found where Great-grandpa dug
was the many-facet thrill and vantage of remoteness.
Sometimes the whole forest seemed to river
up and over my lookout and burn
vivid, then drain into the present.
I listened, close to the new sky.

SECRET PLEASURES

The sourwood sprouts are long
as flyrods in the field we turned-out
years ago. Its soil had worn
so thin the weeds runted and rocks,
boiled up by frost, began to cobble-over
bare spots and gather in the washes.
Erosion left the ground in swells like graves.
Our granary's now the weathered humps
of clay from which we took
the syrup and left
a fragrant dust. Let it
scab and fur over on its own
and offer no crop bigger than dew
and the beadwork of berrypicking.
My secret pleasure: to come and watch
these shoots work up
their honey from bitter clay.
Lichen gardens improve the scars,
patching over history. I offer
the land my leisure.

DEN TREE

When a black bear finds his niche
several stories up in the throat
of a gutted spruce on the Smokies he'll
wrap there in acorn fat and drowse away while

the hunters and their hounds
trouble the thickets.
Shifts and turns like an eyeball
within the wooden socket,

blind to the distant philately of fields
but foraging the cubic lightyears
and focusing on dreams of honey,
trout gold, his body sealed by

a fecal plug. The dead hulk creaks like
a rotten ship and stirs, stack
filling with ice.
Banked as a single coal

and wadded in the tight chamber
he stinks everything around his elevation,
keeping squirrels away from the orifice,
and woodpeckers. A dove nests

in the hollow stub at the tip and calls
through the gray morning.
He will hear that lovesong
lighting his new hunger.

DEVIL'S COURTHOUSE

From their towns along the Little Tennessee
and its feeder creeks, the Cherokee
would make their hunting forays into
the high mountains to
the east, reaching in late summer the cool
peaks of the Plott Balsams and Pisgah —
ranges too misty capped and sacred to live in,
ridges they crossed annually,
their trails seasonal streams that ran
dry except autumn, and the campgrounds
along the upper creeks cluttered with weeds
and fallen limbs. The most terrible
summit of all
they named this crumbling rockface above
the pinkbeds and stayed miles
from its fogs and unseasonal lightnings.
Among the balds and fire-scald knobs only
it had kept a scalp of spruce.
Anyone climbing up there would be
thrown by awful winds into the sky.
Medicine men near the base
could pitch bits of fur and birds and blessed
leaves into the updrafts to be shot
into rare heights and spun
in ceiling thermals. If the gifts fell
somewhere below and were found
the hunt would fail
and it was wise to go back at once
to the hoe farms along the banks to the west.

But if they vanished into the welkin
it meant the offering
was taken and the autumn hunt might prosper.
Told of its efficacy the whites
named the rock Devil's Courthouse for
the nature of the judgements handed down
from its ugly silence
and the nature of their fear.

TRASH

When a pentecost
takes the leaves and dust,
electrifying grit
and boring an eye
in gravity,
the brush spouts
seeds and straw
exhilarating high in a column,
flushing and mounting,
while oaks on nearby
cliffs
stand rooted, unmoved.

PRAYING THROUGH

Keep in mind the hogcalls
and bakesales left
behind, the stink of riverbeds

and shackly log bridges
over your creek.
The shivering is a way

of staying warm.
Don't go for the
summit sting, but carefully

as a trapper gathering rainwater
from the leaves for coffee.
Watch the ceiling wind

carve flat
the bottoms of a cloud flotilla.
Fire is hidden in cool rock,

whole libretti of
burnings that spare
only springs and the waterfall's

libation of smoke.
Autumn pops its
mushrooms on the pasture.

The detours guide,
the side trips and deadends
like pruning

strengthen and confirm the main
stalk of your going out.
The dirt tribulates with rock

and mud, digressing into hollows.
You could get there drunk
or by rhetoric, but without

knowing the terrain for
several sleeps between
the foothills and the barren peak.

The text of this book was set in Californian, designed in 1938 by Frederic W. Goudy for the University of California Press and often considered his best type design. The original printing was done by Heritage Printers using monotype matrices on loan from the University of California and used with their permission. This later printing uses the digital version of this typeface.

The title was lettered by Stephen Harvard.